The Boston Massacre

by Michael Burgan

Content Adviser: Dr. Alan Rogers, History Department Chair,
Boston College, Boston, Massachusetts

Reading Adviser: Susan Kesselring, M.A., Literacy Educator,
Rosemount-Apple Valley-Eagan (Minnesota) School District

COMPASS POINT BOOKS
MINNEAPOLIS, MINNESOTA

Compass Point Books
3109 West 50th Street, #115
Minneapolis, MN 55410

Visit Compass Point Books on the Internet at *www.compasspointbooks.com*
or e-mail your request to *custserv@compasspointbooks.com*

On the cover: British troops fight American colonists in the Boston Massacre.

Stock Montage/Getty Images, cover, 19, 29; Prints Old and Rare, back cover (far left); Library of Congress, back cover, 21; North Wind Picture Archives, 4, 8, 33, 35, 37, 38; Stock Montage, 5, 7, 9, 15, 30; Bettmann/Corbis, 6; Mary Evans Picture Library, 10, 25; MPI/Getty Images, 12, 18, 24, 31, 32; Hulton Archive/Getty Images, 13; John Fitzgerald Kennedy Library, Boston, 16; Collection of The New-York Historical Society, 76738d, 17; Richard T. Nowitz, 20; Courtesy, American Antiquarian Society, 23; Lee Snider/Corbis, 34; Kevin Fleming/Corbis, 41.

Creative Director: Terri Foley
Managing Editor: Catherine Neitge
Editor: Brenda Haugen
Photo Researcher: Marcie C. Spence
Designer: Bradfordesign, Inc./Les Tranby
Educational Consultant: Diane Smolinski
Cartographer: XNR Productions, Inc.

Library of Congress Cataloging-in-Publication Data
Burgan, Michael.
  The Boston Massacre / by Michael Burgan.
    p. cm. — (We the people)
Includes bibliographical references and index.
Audience: Grades 4-6.
ISBN 0-7565-0832-0 (hardcover)
1. Boston Massacre, 1770—Juvenile literature. I. Title. II. We the people (Series) (Compass Point Books)
E215.4.B87 2004
973.3'113—dc22   2004016308

TABLE OF CONTENTS

A BLOODY NIGHT

People in Boston, Massachusetts, were unhappy. Since 1765, the city had been the center of protests against the British for the taxes it charged its 13 American colonies.

British troops enter Boston to maintain order.

British leaders decided they needed to send troops to protect government officials there and to restore order. In 1768, British soldiers arrived in Boston Harbor and camped in the city.

The troops' arrival angered many Bostonians. The British had never placed troops in the

4

A fight breaks out between British soldiers, called redcoats, and Bostonians.

city before. To many residents, the soldiers were another
sign that Parliament did not respect the colonists' rights.
Some Bostonians began insulting the troops when they
saw them in the streets. At times, fistfights erupted
between the colonists and these British troops.

AMERICANS!
BEAR IN REMEMBRANCE
The HORRID MASSACRE!
Perpetrated in King-ſtreet, BOSTON,
New-England,
On the Evening of March the Fifth, 1770,
When FIVE of your fellow countrymen,
GRAY, MAVERICK, CALDWELL, ATTUCKS,
and CARR,
Lay wallowing in their Gore!
Being baſely, and moſt inhumanly
MURDERED!
And SIX others badly WOUNDED!
By a Party of the XXIXth Regiment,
Under the command of Capt. Tho. Preſton.
REMEMBER!
That Two of the MURDERERS
Were convicted of MANSLAUGHTER!
By a Jury, of whom I ſhall ſay
NOTHING,
Branded in the hand!
And diſmiſſed,
The others were ACQUITTED,
And their Captain PENSIONED!
Alſo,
BEAR IN REMEMBRANCE
That on the 22d Day of February, 1770
The infamous
EBENEZER RICHARDSON, Informer,
And tool to Miniſterial hirelings,
Moſt barbarouſly
MURDERED
CHRISTOPHER SEIDER,
An innocent youth!
Of which crime he was found guilty
By his Country
On Friday April 20th, 1770;
But remained Unſentenced
On Saturday the 22d Day of February, 1772,
When the GRAND INQUEST
For Suffolk county,
Were informed, at requeſt,
By the Judges of the Superior Court,
That EBENEZER RICHARDSON'S Caſe
Then lay before his MAJESTY.
Therefore ſaid Richardſon
This day, MARCH FIFTH! 1772,
Remains UNHANGED!!!
Let THESE things be told to Poſterity!
And handed down
From Generation to Generation,
'Till Time ſhall be no more!
Forever may AMERICA be preſerved,
From weak and wicked monarchs,
Tyrannical Miniſters,
Abandoned Governors,
Their Underlings and Hirelings!
And may the
Machinations of artful, deſigning wretches,
Who would ENSLAVE THIS People,
Come to an end,
Let their NAMES and MEMORIES
Be buried in eternal oblivion,
And the PRESS,
For a SCOURGE to Tyrannical Rulers,
Remain FREE.

Part of a document for the Library of Massachusetts describing the Boston Massacre.

On March 5, 1770, the hatred some Bostonians felt toward the British soldiers led to violence and turned deadly. A mob insulted a British guard, then threw snowballs at him. As the crowd grew, more troops arrived to help the soldier. One soldier fired his gun. Both citizens and soldiers shouted, and several more shots followed. In the end, the British killed five Boston residents and wounded six more.

The citizens of Boston called the bloodshed the Boston Massacre. Samuel Adams was a leader of the residents who opposed the British. He tried to use the massacre to convince more colonists to hate the British officials.

UNPOPULAR TAXES

The colonists' relationship with Great Britain had been complicated in the years leading up to the Boston Massacre. Before 1763 and the French and Indian War, the relationship between Britain and the American colonies had been quite calm. This war was fought mainly by England and France, but both countries had the help of allies. With its victory, Great Britain took France's possessions in North America. These included lands east of the Mississippi River that bordered the American colonies. The colonists sometimes fought with Native Americans in that region. The British decided to send troops there to stop the fighting.

George Washington raises a British flag after a battle in the French and Indian War.

7

King George III reigned from 1760 to 1820.

King George III of Great Britain and his lawmakers in Britain's Parliament decided that the Americans should pay taxes to support these troops. In 1764, Parliament passed the Sugar Act. It placed duties on molasses. The next year, the lawmakers approved the Stamp Act. This law made the colonists pay a tax on almost every kind of paper item they used. The tax applied to newspapers, business papers, legal documents— even playing cards.

Boston colonists read the Stamp Act in 1765.

9

King George III opens Parliament with members of both houses attending.

Some American merchants complained about the Sugar Act, but most accepted it. They knew Parliament had a legal right to control trade across the British Empire. Collecting taxes on goods was one way to influence what was bought and sold. However, the Stamp Act's purpose was to raise money by taxing activities that took place only within the colonies. Many Americans believed no government could pass this kind of tax unless the voters or their elected representatives approved it. Under British law, there could be "no taxation without representation." Since the colonists did not have any representatives in Parliament, many of them believed the Stamp Act was illegal.

The Stamp Act led to violent protests in Boston and other American cities. Angry crowds destroyed property and threatened the commissioners who were supposed to collect the taxes. Massachusetts governor Francis Bernard wrote that during the Boston riots, the crowd broke into one house "and tore it all to pieces."

11

Early in 1766, Parliament decided to repeal the Stamp Act. However, at the same time, Parliament declared it could pass future taxes on the colonists without their consent.

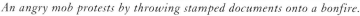
An angry mob protests by throwing stamped documents onto a bonfire.

THE TOWNSHEND ACTS

In 1767, a British official named Charles Townshend asked Parliament to place new taxes on the colonies. The goods taxed included paint, glass, and tea. Members of Parliament were angry with the colonists for their resistance to the Stamp Act. These new taxes would be a way to punish the colonists for their actions.

Parliament also set up the American Board of Custom Commissioners. Its job was to make sure

Charles Townshend

13

laws against smuggling were followed. It also collected the new duties. The board worked from the city of Boston, since many smugglers operated there. Parliament members believed that if the board was successful in stopping smuggling in Boston, other colonial cities would follow the trade laws, too.

Another law set up new admiralty courts. These courts handled crimes committed at sea. Admiralty courts used only judges and did not have juries. In the past, juries in Boston had let accused smugglers go free.

Together, these new laws were called the Townshend Acts. In Boston, many colonists quickly protested the acts, particularly the taxes. They argued that Parliament should not pass any duties or any other tax without the consent of the colonies.

Samuel Adams and others called on all the colonies to boycott certain British goods.

14

Massachusetts lawmakers also sent a letter inviting all of the colonies to join them in asking the king to repeal the Townshend Acts. The British government had ordered Massachusetts not to send the letter, but the Massachusetts lawmakers disobeyed this order. Francis Bernard, the appointed governor of

Samuel Adams

Massachusetts, then shut down the General Court.

As the Massachusetts lawmakers worked to get the taxes repealed, other colonists were active in the streets. In 1765, patriot leaders had formed the Sons of Liberty. This group led the public protests against the Stamp Act. Now the Sons threatened to use violence again to force Great Britain to repeal the Townshend Acts. In March 1768, a group armed with clubs paraded in front of a custom commissioner's home. Another time, the Sons removed cargo from a ship before the duty on it was paid.

Governor Bernard and the customs commissioners worried that the Sons might spark

Massachusetts Governor Francis Bernard

16

NEW-YORK, July 7, 1769.

AT this alarming Crisis when we are threatened with a De-privation of those invaluable Rights, which our Ancestors purchased with their Blood----Rights, which as Men, we derive from Nature; as Englishmen, have secured to us by our excellent Constitution; and which once torn from us, will in all Probability never be restored. At this important Time, when we are exerting every legal Effort to preserve to Ourselves and Posterity the complete and undisturbed Enjoyment of them, it is of the last Conse-quence to act with Vigilance and Unanimity. It must appear obvious to every unprejudiced Mind, that Supineness would prove as fatal to us, as a Disunion; and therefore, the more effectually to guard against both----A Number of the Inhabitants of this City, have deter-mined to drop all Party Distinction that may have originated from a Difference in Sentiments in other Matters---to form Ourselves into a Society, under the general and honourable Appellation, of the UNITED SONS OF LIBERTY,---and strictly to adhere to the following *RESOLUTIONS*,

I. To hold a general Meeting on the first Monday Evening in every Month, at the House of Mr. De La Montagne.

II. To convene occasionally if Circumstances occur to render it necessary.

III. That we will Support the constitutional Measures entered into by the Merchants, Traders, and other Inhabitants of this City.

IV. The grand Design of this Association being to Support the Measures entered into by the Merchants, Traders, and other Inhabi-tants of this City---That, we will not in any Manner whatever coun-teract the Designs of either Committee, but contribute to the effectual Execution of them, by all legal Means in our Power.

V. That we will not knowingly purchase from, nor sell, to any Per-son or Persons who shall violate the Non-importation Agreement.

VI. That we will neither let Houses to, nor hire them from. That we will not employ, nor be employed by, nor in anywise hold Con-nection in Trade with, those who violate the Agreement, or with such as shall Countenance their base Conduct, by dealing with them.

VII. That we do steadily and invariably pursue such Measures, and such only, as shall appear best calculated to promote the general Good of the Colonies. That the sole End of the UNITED SONS OF LIBERTY, is to secure their common Rights---That the Object we have principally in View, is a repeal of the Acts imposing Duties on Paper, Glass, &c. and that we will not as a Society under the said Ap-pellation, engage in any other Matter whatever.

N. B. The United Sons of Liberty, are to hold a Meeting on Monday Evening next, precisely at Seven o'Clock, at the House of Mr. De La Montagne; and do hereby publicly invite every Lover of constitutional Freedom, to meet with them at the above-mentioned Time and Place.

The Sons of Liberty put pressure on merchants to respond to the Townshend Acts.

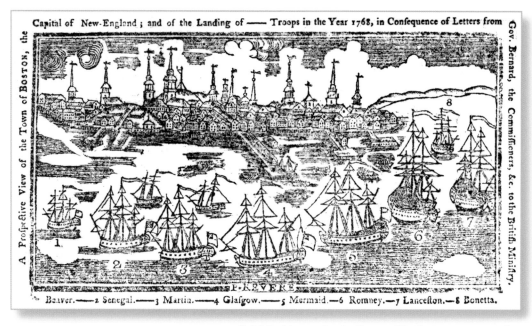

British ships arrive in Boston Harbor to restore order.

even larger protests. Help seemed to arrive when the *Romney,* a British warship, sailed into Boston Harbor. However, its presence only added to the troubles. The *Romney*'s captain began forcing some colonists to serve as sailors. This practice was called impressment. The British officer ignored the fact that impressment was illegal. This made the colonists angry.

In June 1768, the Bostonians' anger boiled over into violence. The customs officials worked with the captain of the *Romney* to seize a colonial ship called the *Liberty*. Its owner was John Hancock, a wealthy patriot merchant. He had ignored the duties he was supposed to pay on cargo that his ship carried. British sailors arrived to board the *Liberty*. An official report noted that they "found a large mob

John Hancock would later be the first to sign the Declaration of Independence.

assembled armed with stones which they threw." Other protesters stormed the homes of the customs officials and attacked several commissioners.

THE TROOPS ARRIVE

The *Liberty* violence upset Governor Bernard. He feared law and order had broken down and that rioters would be allowed to do whatever they wanted. British officials said "the most daring acts of force and violence" were threatening their control in Boston. During the summer of 1768, Bernard and British officials decided that the government should send troops to Boston.

Today, people still dress as British soldiers to reenact the American Revolution.

Castle William as it looked in the late 1700s

When the patriots heard this news, some said Bostonians should greet them with their guns. Despite the tough talk, in October about 700 British troops arrived peacefully. As fifes and drums played, they paraded to a large field called Boston Common. Because they wore long, red coats, the troops were often called redcoats. Many patriots, however, called them lobsterbacks or simply "lobsters."

More troops arrived the next month. Some were stationed at Castle William, a fort on an island in Boston Harbor. The rest stayed in the city, living in rented buildings. Patriots argued that all the troops should have been on the island. Bostonians did not like the idea of a standing army living among them. In the past, British troops had only come to North America to fight wars. Now they were acting like occupiers who had taken over the city. Samuel Adams feared that the troops might "sooner or later begin to look upon themselves as the *lords* and not the *servants* of the people." The troops, however, had orders not to use deadly force unless Governor Bernard asked them to do so.

Some patriots wanted to make life difficult for the redcoats. The British set up guard stations around the city. The soldiers were supposed to stop and question anyone who passed by. Some residents accused the guards of attacking them during these stops. Some of these charges were not true.

Samuel Adams and other patriots also wrote articles describing the soldiers' actions. In some cases, the articles lied to make the soldiers seem worse than they really were. These articles appeared in many newspapers.

On the whole, however, Boston remained calm. In one instance, residents and soldiers even worked together. When a fire broke out at the local jail, the troops helped the citizens put it out. By June 1769, British officials believed they could safely reduce their forces in Boston. About half of the troops soon left the city.

GROWING TROUBLES

Relations between the residents and the redcoats didn't improve, however. They worsened in some ways. The soldiers sometimes took jobs at local businesses. Bostonians who were out of work were unhappy that some of the British soldiers got the jobs instead of them.

The Boston Chronicle *ran articles from both sides.*

Boston's patriots disliked local residents who supported British officials and the troops. These people were called Tories. One well-known Boston Tory was John Mein. He published a newspaper that insulted the Sons of Liberty and the patriots. In October 1769, a crowd led by

[January, 1770]

[1773(2)]

WILLIAM JACKSON,

an *IMPORTER*; at the

BRAZEN HEAD,

North Side of the **TOWN-HOUSE,**

and Opposite the Town-Pump, in

Corn-hill, **BOSTON.**

It is defired that the Sons and
Daughters of *LIBERTY,*
would not buy any one thing of
him, for in fo doing they will bring
Difgrace upon *themfelves,* and their
Pofterity, for *ever* and *ever,* AMEN.

*A document tells patriots not to buy goods
from a Boston merchant who ignored the
boycott against British products.*

the Sons attacked Mein while he was walking in the streets. Thinking the Sons of Liberty would try to kill him, Mein fled and hid in a British guardhouse. He eventually sneaked out of Boston and went to England.

The patriots also threatened merchants who violated the boycott by buying goods from Great Britain. Young boys threw rocks at these merchants' windows and dirt at the customers who entered their shops. In February 1770, a Tory named Ebenezer Richardson confronted a crowd of boys that was taunting a Tory merchant. The boys then threw sticks and stones at him. Richardson fled into his house, but the angry crowd didn't go away.

24

Christopher Seider is fatally wounded during a Boston protest.

Another man came to help Richardson. The two men stood at an open window holding guns. Richardson fired into the crowd and struck Christopher Seider, an 11-year-old boy. As church bells rang out, more people rushed to the scene. The crowd stormed the house. Richardson swung a sword to keep the crowd away. He yelled, "Damn their blood. I don't care what I've done."

The angry patriots finally captured Richardson. They wanted to kill him on the spot, but one patriot leader convinced them to stop. Within hours of the shooting, Christopher Seider died. On February 26, thousands of residents came out to honor him. More than ever, Bostonians were angry with the Tories and the British.

Trouble stirred again on Friday, March 2. A British soldier named Patrick Walker went looking for work to make some extra money. At a ropewalk, where ropes were made, Walker traded insults with the owner. He left, but returned with a small group of soldiers to fight the rope makers. The workers called for help, and soon more rope makers joined the fight. The colonists drove off the British. Walker returned again, bringing an even larger group of soldiers. Both sides swung fists, clubs, and sticks in the fight that followed. Finally, the soldiers fled.

Neither side, however, was ready to end the battle. A local minister heard that some residents were ready for "fighting it out with the soldiers on Monday."

THE BOSTON MASSACRE

That Monday, March 5, 1770, was a chilly day. Snow from a recent storm still lined the streets. That evening, Private Hugh White was stationed at a guard post on King Street.

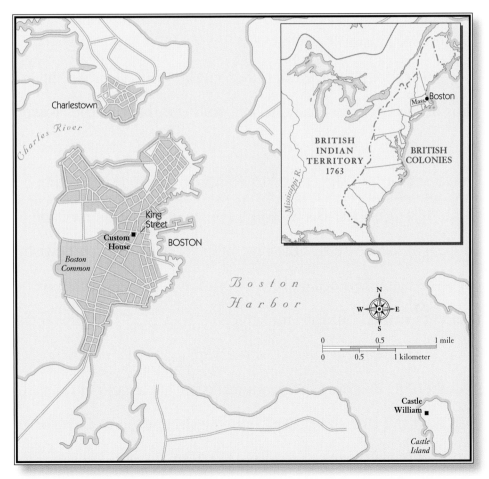

The Custom House is found on King Street in Boston.

27

The post was near the Custom House, where British officials collected duties. Some time after 8 p.m., a few young men approached White and began to taunt him. The soldier grew angry, and he swung his heavy gun. The gun hit one of the boys on the side of his head. A small crowd began to gather. It continued to insult White, calling him a "scoundrel lobster."

As more people gathered around, White climbed the steps of the Custom House so he could stand above the crowd. He loaded his gun and said he would fire if the crowd attacked. One resident told the crowd to go home and to leave White alone. Instead, they threw chunks of ice at the soldier. Angry and frightened, White called for help. Nearby, church bells began to ring. Thinking a fire might have broken out, some residents rushed out into the streets.

At the same time, two other angry crowds had formed elsewhere in Boston. One group carrying sticks and clubs gathered near the British soldiers' housing. In another square, several hundred people listened to a speaker. One witness later said the

Fighting erupts between the soldiers and the colonists.

speaker seemed to be stirring up the crowd's emotions. When he finished speaking, the angry mob headed for King Street.

Fearing the growing crowd on King Street might kill White, some residents told Captain Thomas Preston about the situation. Preston commanded the soldiers on guard duty that night. He thought about what to do and finally took seven men with him to help White.

When he arrived at the scene, Preston asked the crowd to go home. The people ignored him. They threw snowballs and shouted insults. More than 300 Bostonians crowded around the British soldiers.

Some people in the crowd dared the soldiers to fire. "They cannot fire without my orders," Preston told the mob. However, when a club flew through the crowd and struck a soldier, one of the redcoats shouted, "Damn you, fire!" and pulled the trigger on his gun. After a pause, six of the other soldiers fired their guns into the crowd.

Two bullets struck Crispus Attucks. He was a tall man of mixed African and Native American background. Attucks had led a small group of

Crispus Attucks

seamen into the larger crowd. He had taunted the British, and one witness said Attucks had struck the soldier who fired the first shot.

Attucks was the first patriot to die that night. James Caldwell and Sam Gray also were shot dead. Another bullet bounced before

Hours to the Gates of this City many Thousands of our brave Brethren in the Country, deeply affected with our Distresses, and to whom we are greatly obliged on this Occasion—No one knows where this would have ended, and what important Consequences even to the whole British Empire might have followed, which our Moderation & Loyalty upon so trying an Occasion, and our Faith in the Commander's Assurances have happily prevented.

Last Thursday, agreeable to a general Request of the Inhabitants, and by the Consent of Parents and Friends, were carried to their Grave in Succession, the Bodies of *Samuel Gray*, *Samuel Maverick*, *James Caldwell*, and *Crispus Attucks*, the unhappy Victims who fell in the bloody Massacre of the Monday Evening preceeding !

On this Occasion most of the Shops in Town were shut, all the Bells were ordered to toll a solemn Peal, as were also those in the neighboring Towns of Charlestown Roxbury, &c. The Procession began to move between the Hours of 4 and 5 in the Afternoon ; two of the unfortunate Sufferers, viz. Mess. *James Caldwell* and *Crispus Attucks*, who were Strangers, borne from Faneuil-Hall,

The obituaries of four of the men killed in the fighting

hitting Samuel Maverick. He died later, as did Patrick Carr, an Irish immigrant. Several more people lay wounded on the street.

Angry and confused, Preston yelled at his men. He demanded to know why the men had fired. They told him they had heard someone give that command. The crowd carried off the wounded and the dead, and more Bostonians filled King Street. Preston ordered his men back to their guardhouse.

News of the killings, called the Boston Massacre, spread quickly. Around the city, residents attacked some British officers who were out on the streets. Fearing even more violence, acting Massachusetts governor Thomas Hutchinson went to King Street and spoke to the crowd. He promised them that Preston and the other soldiers would be arrested and brought to trial. The crowd finally began to head home.

Thomas Hutchinson served as governor of Massachusetts after Francis Bernard.

THE TRIAL

The next day, about 3,000 people attended a town meeting
to discuss the massacre. They formed a committee that was
led by Samuel Adams. The committee demanded that
Governor Hutchinson send the remaining British troops
to Castle William. Hutchinson agreed.

Samuel Adams warns the governor that more trouble will come if soldiers stay in Boston.

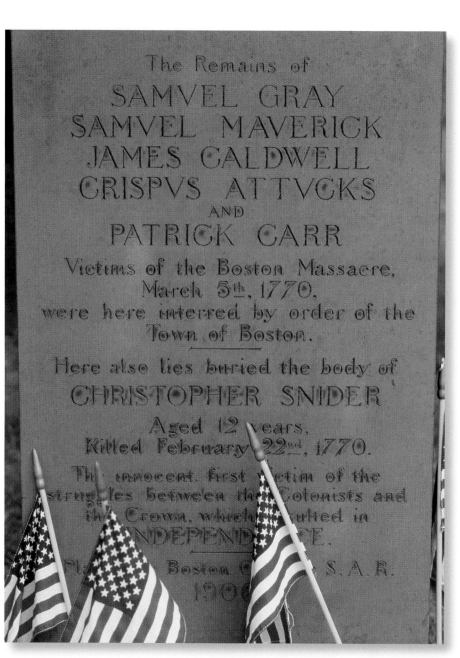

A marker for the victims of the Boston Massacre stands in the Granary Burial Ground.

A few days later, an even larger crowd attended the funeral for four of the massacre victims. At another town meeting, Bostonians asked the General Court to set up a monument to honor the dead.

The patriot leaders published a report that included eyewitness accounts of what had happened on March 5. The report helped stir up anger toward the British soldiers involved in the massacre.

Just a week after the massacre, Preston and the eight British soldiers were officially charged for their roles in the killings. They had already found lawyers to defend them. The

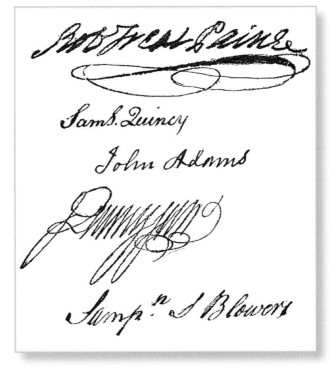

The signatures of all the lawyers involved in the trial

most important of these was John Adams, a cousin of Samuel Adams. John was a patriot, but he also believed everyone had the right to a fair trial, including British soldiers.

In October 1770, Captain Preston's trial began. He was charged with causing the murder of the five dead men because he had ordered his men to fire. John Adams argued that Preston had not given that command. Many people in the mob yelled for the troops to fire, but no witness could say for sure that Preston had also yelled "fire." Even if he had given that order, John Adams argued, the mob's actions that night made the soldiers think their lives were at risk. Shooting into the crowd was an act of self-defense, not murder. In the end, the jury found Preston innocent.

The trial of the eight soldiers began on November 27, 1770. Dozens of witnesses appeared. Some confirmed that soldiers had been at the Custom House when the shootings occurred on March 5. Some

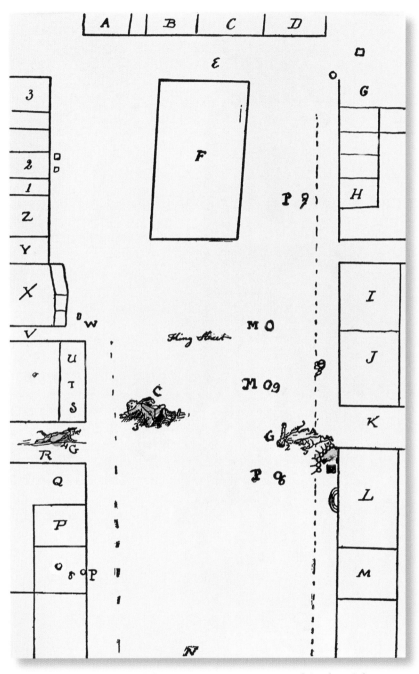

Paul Revere's drawing of the Boston Massacre was used in the trial.

said many people that night carried sticks and clubs. Other witnesses recalled that members of the crowd had screamed at the soldiers and dared them to fire their guns.

When John Adams spoke to the jury, he stressed that the soldiers had fired in self-defense. The crowd that confronted Private White and the other troops was "an unlawful assembly." The rioters threw bricks and swung clubs, trying to hurt the soldiers. "The law is clear," Adams said, "they [the soldiers] had a right to kill in their own defense."

John Adams would become the second president.

Once again, the jury agreed with Adams. It found six of the soldiers not guilty. Two were found guilty of the lesser crime of manslaughter. This meant they killed someone but didn't mean to do it. Those two soldiers faced execution for their crimes, but an old English legal custom spared their lives. The men claimed "benefit of clergy." This law had once been used to protect priests from punishment. In English courts, benefit of clergy also applied to people who could read. The two soldiers proved they could read and were not killed. Instead, each was branded with hot metal on his right thumb as punishment for his crime.

After the trials were done, Samuel Adams wrote a series of articles about the Boston Massacre. He did not want Americans to forget that British policy had caused it.

In later years, Samuel Adams and other patriots gave speeches on March 5. They reminded Bostonians of the blood that had been shed because of the British.

The massacre convinced the British that troops in Boston were more likely to start trouble than end it. The massacre also helped convince patriots throughout the American colonies that King George III's goal was tyranny over them.

The Boston Massacre was part of a series of conflicts between the Americans and the British. These conflicts eventually led to the Revolutionary War and freedom for the colonies from British rule.

Today, a circle of cobblestones marks the site of the Boston Massacre.

41

GLOSSARY

allies—people or countries who agree to help each other in times of trouble

boycott—refusal to buy certain goods

duties—taxes placed on goods brought into a country from another country

Parliament—the part of the British government that makes laws

patriot—an American who opposed British policies before and during the American Revolution

repeal—overturn a law

representatives—people chosen to support the interests of a larger group

rioters—a group of people who become violent in a public area

ropewalk—place where ropes are made

smuggling—illegally bringing goods into a port

standing army—a permanent army that serves during peacetime as well as wartime

DID YOU KNOW?

- Before the Boston Massacre trials, Parliament repealed the Townshend Acts, except for the duty on tea. That tax eventually led to the Boston Tea Party, another important event on the road to the Revolutionary War.

- By British law, a public official had to read the Riot Act before soldiers could fire on rioters. The Riot Act ordered the crowd to go home. Today, the expression "read the riot act" is still used, meaning to warn someone to stop doing something bad.

- Boston is sometimes called the Cradle of Liberty because so many of the important events that led to the Revolutionary War happened in and around the city.

IMPORTANT DATES

Timeline

1763	Great Britain wins the French and Indian War, gaining new lands in North America.
1765	Boston residents protest the Stamp Act, which taxes paper goods used in the colonies.
1766	Parliament repeals the Stamp Act.
1767	Parliament passes the Townshend Acts, which include new taxes on the colonies.
1768	Bostonians protest the new taxes and threaten the commissioners who are supposed to collect them; the British send troops to Boston to restore order.
1770	In February, Ebenezer Richardson kills 11-year-old Christopher Seider. On March 2, British soldiers and Boston workers fight in the streets. On March 5, troops fire on a large crowd and kill five Americans. The event is soon called the Boston Massacre. In October, John Adams convinces a jury that Captain Thomas Preston did not order the troops to fire. The next month, a jury finds six soldiers innocent of murder and two soldiers guilty of a lesser crime.

IMPORTANT PEOPLE

JOHN ADAMS (1735–1826)
Lawyer who defended the British soldiers accused of killing five Americans

SAMUEL ADAMS (1722–1803)
Leader of the Bostonians who opposed British policies before and after the Boston Massacre

CRISPUS ATTUCKS (?1723–1770)
African-American sailor who was the first person killed during the Boston Massacre

FRANCIS BERNARD (1712–1779)
Governor of Massachusetts when British troops first arrived in Boston

THOMAS HUTCHINSON (1711–1780)
Acting governor of Massachusetts during the Boston Massacre

THOMAS PRESTON (1722–1798)
British captain who commanded the troops that took part in the Boston Massacre

CHARLES TOWNSHEND (1725–1767)
British official who ordered new taxes for the American colonies in 1767

WANT TO KNOW MORE?

At the Library

Bohannon, Lisa Frederiksen. *The American Revolution.* Minneapolis: Lerner
  Publications, 2004.

Burgan, Michael. *Colonial and Revolutionary Times.* New York: Franklin
  Watts, 2003.

Irvin, Benjamin. *Samuel Adams: Son of Liberty, Father of Revolution.* New
  York: Oxford University Press, 2002.

Mattern, Joanne. *The Cost of Freedom: Crispus Attucks and the Boston
  Massacre.* New York: Rosen Publishing Group, 2003.

On the Web

For more information on *the Boston Massacre,* use FactHound

to track down Web sites related to this book.

1. Go to *www.facthound.com.*

2. Type in a search word related to this book
   or this book ID: 0756508320.

3. Click on the *Fetch It* button.

Your trusty FactHound will fetch the best Web sites for you!

On the Road

Boston Historical Society and Museum

Old State House
206 Washington St.
Boston, MA 02109-1713
To see exhibits on the
Boston Massacre

The Freedom Trail

The Freedom Trail Foundation
99 Chauncy St., Suite 401
Boston, MA 02111
To learn about the Freedom Trail
and visit where Boston residents
led American independence

Look for more We the People books about this era:

The Battle of Lexington and Concord

The Bill of Rights

The Boston Tea Party

The Declaration of Independence

*Great Women of the American
   Revolution*

The Minutemen

Monticello

Mount Vernon

Paul Revere's Ride

The U.S. Constitution

Valley Forge

A complete list of We the People titles is available on our Web site:
www.compasspointbooks.com

INDEX

About the Author

Michael Burgan is a freelance writer of books for children and adults. A history graduate of the University of Connecticut, he has written more than 80 fiction and nonfiction children's books for various publishers. For adult audiences, he has written news articles, essays, and plays. Michael Burgan is a recipient of an Educational Press Association of America award and belongs to the Society of Children's Book Writers and Illustrators.